Surviving
the Holidays

SURVIVAL GUIDE

For more information:
Church Initiative
PO Box 1739
Wake Forest, NC 27588-1739

Phone: 800-489-7778 (US and Canada); 919-562-2112 (local and international)
Fax: 919-562-2114
Email: info@churchinitiative.org
Web address: churchinitiative.org, divorcecare.org

Welcome

The holiday season has begun. This might be the first holiday after your separation or divorce, or maybe it's the second, third, or beyond.

In the coming days, you are going to be facing some tough emotions. And due to the nature of Thanksgiving and Christmas—with their focus on family, social events, yearly traditions, expectations, and "cheer"—the emotions can blindside you.

You can lessen the emotional impact by knowing what to expect and being prepared.

Surviving the Holidays is here to help.

Today you will watch a video, be part of a discussion group, and receive a Survival Guide with daily encouragement and helpful exercises for the days ahead.

These tools will enable you not only to survive the coming holidays, but also to face them with a measure of peace and assurance.

In His love,

Steve Grissom
DivorceCare founder and president
divorcecare.org

Contents

Holiday Survival Guide:

Chapter 1 What to Do with Your Holiday Emotions 5

Chapter 4   Surviving Thanksgiving and Christmas Day 51

What to Expect Today

You may be uncertain of what to expect today and a bit apprehensive about being here. You won't regret coming!

Surviving the Holidays consists of three important components. All three can help you heal and prepare you to face the coming holiday season.

Video

Today you'll watch a video where you'll meet counselors, pastors, and "real-life" people who have experienced a marital breakup or another life tragedy. These people share honestly about:

- Being prepared for surprising emotions that may hit over the holidays
- What to do about traditions and other coming changes
- How to handle holiday parties and invitations
- How to survive potentially awkward moments with other people
- Where to find comfort, strength, and hope in a seemingly hopeless time

Use the note-taking section in this Survival Guide to jot down comments and questions while viewing the video.

Discussion

After the video, you'll have the chance to talk with others who have experienced a separation or divorce, discuss what you've learned on the video, and ask questions about any concerns you have. Please understand you do not have to share during the discussion time, but you will still benefit from listening to others.

Personal reflection

Your Survival Guide has practical strategies, words of strength and encouragement, valuable tips, and charts and exercises for daily survival through the holiday season. Take this book home and commit to reading one or two pages per day between now and Christmas. You might choose to read them in the order they are written, or you may skip around and choose your own order.

Also visit **divorcecare.org/holidays**, where you'll find helpful articles and video clips on holiday survival after a separation or divorce.

Surviving the Holidays is a special holiday program produced by DivorceCare, a divorce recovery support group program. We encourage you to find and attend a DivorceCare group (**divorcecare.org**). Online groups are also available.

Meet the Cohosts

Steve Grissom, founder and president of Church Initiative, knows firsthand the devastation of divorce. After experiencing healing from his own divorce, he followed God's calling over the years to create and produce a support group resource that churches could use to help people hurting from broken marriages. Steve remarried, and he and his wife, Cheryl, designed and developed the DivorceCare program. Today DivorceCare, as well as Church Initiative's other care group resources (DivorceCare for Kids, Single & Parenting, and GriefShare), are found in thousands of churches worldwide.

Denise Hildreth Jones, author and speaker, is founder of Reclaiming Hearts Ministries. After 13 years of marriage, Denise's painful journey through divorce brought her to a place of heartbreak, fear, and disappointment. God's healing from this hurt formed the basis of her book *Reclaiming Your Heart: A Journey Back to Laughing, Loving, and Living* and ignited her passion for helping others reclaim their hearts. Denise remarried, and she and her husband, Philly, now lead Reclaiming Hearts Ministries, offering Bible studies and events that challenge people to be transformed by God's Word.

Meet the Experts

Sabrina Black is a counselor, speaker, author, professor, and life coach. She is president of the National Biblical Counselors Association and clinical director of Abundant Life Counseling Center in Detroit, MI. **abundantlifecounseling.webs.com**

Elsa Kok Colopy is a speaker and the author of *Settling for Less Than God's Best?: A Relationship Checkup for Single Women; A Woman Who Hurts, A God Who Heals*; and *The Single Mom's Guide to Finding Joy in the Chaos*. She was a single parent for 12 years after her divorce. **elsakokcolopy.com**

Dr. Zoricelis Davila is a licensed professional counselor with a doctorate in counseling education and supervision. She travels internationally to teach on the challenges of family, spirituality, and mental health and has authored books on the topic of family crisis prevention.

Ron L. Deal is a licensed marriage and family therapist with an expertise in blended families. He is founder of Smart Stepfamilies and director of FamilyLife Blended, and he's authored numerous works on stepfamily living, including the best-selling book *The Smart Stepfamily*. **smartstepfamilies.com**

Omar King is a counselor at Bridgehaven Counseling in Raleigh, NC. He holds a master's of divinity with biblical counseling degree from Southeastern Baptist Theological Seminary.

Melody Lovvorn is a speaker and teacher on marriage, parenting, sexual addiction, and betrayal trauma. After having been divorced herself, she now provides life and marriage coaching, recovery intensives, and parenting solutions through the nonprofit Undone Redone. **undoneredone.com**

Dr. Linda Mintle has been in clinical practice as a licensed therapist for 30 years. As a best-selling author, she has written 20 books, including *I Married You, Not Your Family*. Known as "The Relationship Doctor," she is a national speaker and news consultant and hosts her own show on Faith Radio. **drlindamintle.com**

Dr. Elias Moitinho is professor of counseling at Liberty University in Virginia. He has years of experience serving as a pastor, counselor, professor, and the director of a Christian counseling center. His website provides videos and instructional articles for personal growth in life, marriage, and family. **motivationandgrowth.com**

Dr. Ramon Presson is a licensed marriage and family therapist in Tennessee. He is founder of The Marriage Counseling Center of Franklin. He has also authored several books, including *When Will My Life Not Suck?: Authentic Hope for the Disillusioned*. **ramonpressontherapy.com**

Georgia Shaffer is a professional certified coach and licensed psychologist. While battling a recurrence of breast cancer, Georgia went through the loss of her marriage and her job. She wrote *Taking Out Your Emotional Trash* and *A Gift of Mourning Glories*, which provide personal guidance for rebuilding after loss. **georgiashaffer.com**

Leslie Vernick is a licensed clinical social worker, national speaker, and relationship coach with expertise in marriage improvement and conflict resolution. Her books include *The Emotionally Destructive Marriage* and *How to Live Right When Your Life Goes Wrong*. **leslievernick.com**

Dr. Stephen Viars is pastor of Faith Church and a counselor at Faith Biblical Counseling Ministries in Lafayette, IN. He speaks at conferences, colleges, and seminaries in the US and abroad. He authored *Putting Your Past in Its Place: Moving Forward in Freedom and Forgiveness*.

About DivorceCare

DivorceCare is a network of divorce support groups for people facing a separation or divorce. After today's holiday seminar, you will find it helpful and encouraging to attend a weekly DivorceCare group.

A marital breakup is a painful, stressful experience. It's a confusing time when you feel isolated and have lots of questions about issues you've never faced before. DivorceCare groups meet weekly to help you face these challenges and move toward rebuilding your life.

You'll discover there are people who understand your emotional upheaval and pain. You'll find a safe place where you can express your emotions, or where you can choose to just sit quietly and process what you're learning.

You'll learn helpful, practical information that will help you recover from your separation or divorce.

DivorceCare topics include:

- How to handle the loneliness, depression, anger, hurt, etc.
- Where to find the strength to go on
- Ways to help your children
- Practical info on financial survival
- What the Bible says about divorce, forgiveness, reconciliation, single sexuality, and other divorce-related topics

A DivorceCare group includes a weekly video seminar, discussion group, and take-home book. The videos feature respected counselors and teachers and "real-life" people who share their struggles after separation or divorce and what has helped them. After viewing the video with your group, you'll spend time as a small group discussing the concepts on the video and how they apply to your day-to-day life.

Taking the step of walking into a DivorceCare session is hard, but it may be one of the best decisions you'll make.

DivorceCare groups are found in thousands of locations across the US, Canada, and several other countries. To find a group near you, go to **divorcecare.org**. Online groups are also available!

You can enter your postal code or city for a list of DivorceCare groups meeting nearby. Or you can call the DivorceCare offices at 800-489-7778 for help in finding a group near you.

divorcecare.org, 800-489-7778

DIVORCE*Care* Surviving the Holidays

What to Do with Guilt and Regrets

If only I'd been more attentive … nicer … taken better care of myself. Then I wouldn't be alone this holiday.

Because of the divorce, my kids have very few gifts under the tree.

Why did I make those wrong choices? It's changed everything.

You are not alone if regrets, guilt, and even shame are plaguing you this holiday season. Guilt is a common feeling after the loss of a marriage. But God offers you something that will help you find peace and freedom from your guilt.

Please understand first, though, that sometimes people feel guilty when they shouldn't. Your feelings of guilt might have nothing to do with wrongdoing on your part; they are more like regrets.*

If the guilt you feel is appropriate, or your wrong choices caused the breakup, don't despair! Christmas reminds us that God loves us and is willing to forgive us. He doesn't want you overwhelmed by shame, discouragement, or self-condemnation.

Even if you did not want your marriage to end and fought to keep your family together, you still have areas in your life where you need God's forgiveness.

---

* Ask trusted friends, a pastor, and/or a counselor whether they think your guilt is unfounded or is based on something you need forgiveness for. Getting multiple perspectives helps.

Because no one is perfect. The Bible says that "all have sinned and fall short of the glory of God" (Romans 3:23).

The free gifts of forgiveness and perfect standing

You're probably thinking, "I'm hurting enough right now as it is, and you want to talk about my sin?" Yes, because the consequences of our failures and disobedience are far more serious than people tend to think.

Suppose you've had an attitude with family members who were trying to help this holiday season. Or perhaps you've spoken harshly to your kids or coworkers. Maybe you've tried to get revenge on your spouse for hurting you. Even though those actions and reactions are in some ways understandable, God still doesn't approve of them. In fact, anytime we say, do, or even think anything that is contrary to God's will, we are guilty of sin.

What's more is that the penalty for sin is death, spiritually and eternally: "For the wages of sin is death" (Romans 6:23a). Hopefully now you can see why it's critical to talk about your sin.

Now, here's some good news ...

Out of His love for you, God offers you the free gifts of forgiveness and perfect standing in His eyes through His Son. Jesus came to forgive and remove the guilt of all who admit they haven't lived up to God's expectations and who fully depend upon Jesus for help. Jesus, who is sin-free, transfers His perfect standing to everyone who believes that He suffered and died to pay the penalty for his or her sins.

How to receive these gifts

"For he [God] has rescued us from the kingdom of darkness and transferred us into the Kingdom of his dear Son, who purchased our freedom and forgave our sins."

Colossians 1:13–14 NLT

This Christmas season is a good time to make sure you've received the wonderful gifts of forgiveness and perfect standing. You do that by faith, by simply believing you have disobeyed God, acknowledging your need for Christ to die in your place, and agreeing that God should be the one directing your life (1 John 1:9; Romans 10:9–10).

The moment you believe those things, all your sins are forgiven and you are in perfect standing with God:

DIVORCE *Care* **Surviving the Holidays**

"[God] has reconciled you to himself through the death of Christ … and you are holy and blameless as you stand before him without a single fault. But you must continue to believe this truth and stand firmly in it." (Colossians 1:22–23a NLT)

The wrongs you've done should be taken seriously—anything from snide remarks or angry emails to quietly pushing someone's buttons to hurt that person. God has graciously shown us how to deal with our sin so we can experience forgiveness. If you would like to receive the gift of forgiveness and acknowledge Jesus' right to lead you, tell God something like this:

Dear God, I don't always get everything right. In fact, I often stubbornly live life on my own terms. Thank You for helping me to see how wrong that is. And thank You for sending Jesus to suffer and die in my place for my sins. I'm so glad that Christ lived a perfect life for me—and that You accept me as if I've never done anything wrong. You are the one who should direct and guide me. So I resign from calling the shots and submit to Your leadership. Thank You for forgiving me and making me perfect in Your sight. Please help and comfort me as I deal with the pain and confusion of my divorce.

"Yet God freely and graciously declares that we are righteous. He did this through Christ Jesus when he freed us from the penalty for our sins." (Romans 3:24 NLT)

"I love that God has given us a free gift," says counselor Zoricelis Davila, "and it is not something that I have to work to earn. Our forgiveness and our salvation is by grace because God loves us, because He wants to give us that gift."

Christmas can be a time of peace and freedom from guilt for you. Why? Because Christmas is when we celebrate Jesus coming to this earth, the event that made God's gift of forgiveness possible. We celebrate the fact that, through Jesus, we can experience God's peace and forgiveness and be in a relationship with Him, now and eternally. And if you have turned control of your life over to Jesus, that's even more reason to celebrate this holiday season!

> "He has removed our sins as far from us as the east is from the west."
>
> *Psalm 103:12 NLT*

DIVORCE *Care*

Holiday Survival Guide:

Practical helps for the holiday season

In this section of the book you'll find practical tips, words of strength and encouragement, and charts and exercises to help you face and survive the unique stresses of the holiday season. Take this book home and commit to reading one or two pages per day between now and Christmas. You might choose to read them in the order they are written, or you may skip around and choose your own order. Use the video note-taking outline to take notes while viewing the video seminar.

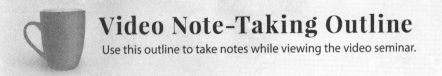

Video Note-Taking Outline

Use this outline to take notes while viewing the video seminar.

Why the Holidays Hurt

Grief doesn't have a statute of limitations

_____

_____

_____

_____

_____

Accept that there will be enjoyable and difficult moments

_____

_____

_____

Holiday Gatherings

Responding to invitations from friends and coworkers

_____

_____

_____

Responding to invitations from family

_____

_____

_____

_____

DIVORCE *Care* Surviving the Holidays

Avoiding Conflicts

Don't put the kids in the middle

_____

_____

_____

_____

Encourage the kids to enjoy time with the other parent

_____

_____

_____

Adjusting the Budget

Focus on memories, not spending

_____

_____

_____

_____

Changes in Traditions

Spend time with others—don't isolate!

_____

_____

_____

_____

Be willing to accept help from others

_____

_____

_____

Give yourself grace

Cut out what do not
have to do.

Give yourself freedom to rest

Remember Holiday Themes

Giving thanks during painful times

helps curb anger + hurts
mind body + outlook
look at all have to
celebrate

Hope in hardship: Christ was born for us

Reason for season
not about me anymore
About family

Hope beyond your current circumstances

Because of Christ
walk w/ God in
our sadness

CHAPTER 1

What to Do with Your Holiday Emotions

Everywhere you look, couples are laughing together at a restaurant, holding hands in the mall, or enjoying a cup of holiday cocoa with their kids. A new wave of emotions washes over you as you consider what you've lost.

What do you do with these emotions? Where do you find the strength to make it through? In this chapter you'll find out:

- What's normal in holiday grief

- How to prepare for emotional ambushes

- How to communicate with people whose well-meaning questions and advice are draining and hurtful

- Where to find the strength to make it through

Survivor Stories

*Sometimes it seems like no one truly understands the tough emotions
of separation or divorce. In this "Survivor Stories" section,
you'll meet people who share some of their struggles over the holidays.*

"It was difficult Christmas shopping and watching TV, because I'd see couples walking around shopping together, doing things, and I would look at them and wonder, 'What do [those women] have that I don't have? What redeeming quality is in them that's not in me? How come her husband can see that in her, whereas my husband can't see that in me?'" – *Jennifer*

"Shortly before Thanksgiving, my wife let me know she was leaving. Instead of dealing with the pain of the holidays, I decided to go to work. Well, that kept expanding. I got to the point where I was like, *I can do more work. I can do more work.* I was avoiding dealing with some of the major issues within myself. This led to me working a lot of time, seven days a week, which I realize now was insane. I was running a treadmill, and I'd put myself on it." – *Wesley*

The Strength to Survive

These short daily readings will help you know what to expect over the holidays and offer encouragement and support in the face of added stress and emotions.

Prepare for Hard-Hitting Moments

"My ex's attorney had a mode of sending me things that would be disturbing on specific dates. I got something right before Christmas. I was served papers on New Year's Eve," shares Susan.

"I had a good Christmas with my family," says Jennifer, "but when I was in my car on my way home, the thought suddenly hit me that I was going home to an empty house. It devastated me."

The situations you'll face during the Thanksgiving and Christmas season—as well as your feelings and responses to them—will be unique. But hearing from others who've made it through the holidays after a separation or divorce will give you an idea of what to expect. And when you have an idea of what to expect, you are less likely to be surprised, which lessens the emotional impact.

"When I got to the New Year's party," says Susan, "it was overwhelming being the single one in a group of five other couples. I did not anticipate it being hard."

Now, you can't prepare for every moment, so please understand that the emotions will come, and when they do come, allow yourself to face them, to let them come. You will also benefit from opening your Bible and echoing the heartfelt prayers you'll find in its pages. The Bible says that God's Word is living and active and always useful. Incorporating Bible verses into your prayers is a powerful practice that brings results—in good and bad times. Here is an example that you will be able to relate to:

"Save me, O God, for the waters have come up to my neck. ... Answer me, LORD, out of the goodness of your love; in your great mercy turn to me. ... Answer me quickly, for I am in trouble." (Psalm 69:1, 16–17b)

God, may Your words and promises in Scripture be my prayer in hard-hitting moments: "Lord, You are always with me; You hold me by my right hand. ... My flesh and my heart may fail, but You are the strength of my heart and my portion forever." (Based on Psalm 73:23, 26)

TAKEAWAY:
- Expect hard-hitting emotions. It won't stop them, but that expectation will help lessen the surprise factor.
- Plan beforehand to ride out the emotions.
- Pray words directly from the Bible. (Consider memorizing verses and/ or getting a Bible app.)

Realistic Expectations

Perhaps you are hoping to re-create a semblance of past holidays in order to feel things are as "normal" as possible. The reality is that things are not the same. Realizing and accepting this will help you to not set yourself up for a fall, and it will enable you to heal.

"Accepting the reality that Christmas and Thanksgiving may never be as they once were is difficult, but the best thing you can be is realistic," advises Laura Petherbridge, Christian author. "What used to be normal is no longer."

Monica shares, "I walked into Christmas thinking it would be the same as what I normally had, and it was so different. I realized my family was way different."

Taking the time to reflect on what your holidays might look like this year will help prepare you for changes to come and help keep you from being blindsided emotionally.*

Consider some of the holiday activities and traditions that are a typical part of your season: What will these activities look like without your former spouse? Which moments are potentially hard-hitting from an emotional standpoint? Also consider the differences in relationships with people you've typically spent time with over the holidays. Perhaps past holidays were spent with in-laws or friends you socialized with as a couple.

As you reflect on differences in the days to come, also reflect on God's promises to you and His unchanging love for you. The Bible says that God loves you deeply; He will take care of you; and He will supply your needs. "Lean into the reality that God loves you," encourages Christian writer Lois Rabey.

"Now let your unfailing love comfort me, just as you promised me." (Psalm 119:76a NLT)

God, help me to face the fact that the holidays this year will be different and to prepare for this reality. I want to be as ready as possible for any emotions and difficult times that come. Thank You for loving me just the way I am and for meeting me right where I am in my pain. When I experience tough moments, teach me to lean into Your love and to know I am accepted and valued there.

TAKEAWAY:
Consider beforehand what your holiday traditions/events might look and feel like without your ex. Having a realistic perspective helps protect you emotionally.

* The "Keep Yourself from Being Blindsided" exercise on page 15 will help you in your reflection process.

Surprised by the Intensity of Your Emotions

"Every place I turned, I would see families together. It's like somebody's punching your heart," says Bill.

"The reality of Christmas for my children without their father at home just smacked me," shares Susan.

Try not to be surprised by your emotions this holiday season. You are grieving not only the loss of a relationship, but also the loss of family traditions and someone to share them with. Tears, sadness, depression, and anger are normal emotions in grief, and you can expect the sights and events of the holidays to trigger them. Let the emotions come (whatever your emotions may be) and find people you can express them with who will support and affirm you.

"It's important that when you experience the loss of your marriage and family structure, that you do process your pain. So don't mask the pain, and don't try to run from the pain," says Sabrina Black.

Facing and expressing your emotions on a daily basis is a helpful (and necessary) process after a separation or divorce.

Counselor Susan Lutz explains, "It's easier to have an honest grief that moves you through your pain by being candid about the fact that it is going to be hard. That's different from feeling panicky and anxious. There is a way to respect and take care of your emotions without letting them paralyze you. You respect something by saying, 'Yes, it's here; it's not going away, but I'm not going through it alone. I have to meet the pain. I have to remember that God is with me.'"

You don't have to and should not face your emotions alone. To rely on yourself for support would be exhausting, to say the least. Surrender your feelings and fears to God today. Read out loud this promise from God to you:

"For I am the LORD your God who takes hold of your right hand and says to you, Do not fear; I will help you." (Isaiah 41:13)

God, how will I handle the emotions that come? I can't do it by myself. But with You, Lord, I am never alone. Help me to know Your strength and comfort, to understand Your love for me and for my family. Please tell me when and how to push into the pain, and guide me through this process.

REFLECT:
What is your process for facing your emotions honestly and expressing them?

TAKEAWAY:

After a marital breakup, it's normal to experience tough, unexpected emotions over the holidays. Respect that you need to lean into and meet those emotions.

Survivor Wisdom

Advice and encouragement from people who know the pain of loss.

QUESTION: Where Do You Find the Strength?

In the Bible
Reading through the Psalms was a tremendous help. – *Sharon*

Psalm 23 really helped me. I tried to pray that and read it again and again. And not just reading it, [but] trying to understand every word that God was telling me through that Psalm. I just held on to His promises. – *Maria*

In God's truth
God is who He says He is, and I am who God says I am. So despite the chaos around me, the fact that I know those two things is a foundation and a security that God's going to walk with me through this and I will come out. – *Susan*

Through prayer and helping others
I got on my knees and I cried out and asked God, "Please give me strength, because I don't even want to move. I don't want to do anything. I don't care about anything." After I released it [to God] and I asked for His help, I realized I had some strength. So I put clothes on, and I went to somebody who had been helping me, and I helped them around the house, which made me feel better. – *Shay*

In God's people and His church
God and the strength the church brought to me was my rock. – *Eddie*

I chose to go to church to allow God to refuel me. I knew that I needed some strength. – *Gracie*

In thankfulness
I decided I was going to walk around the lake, and I was going to name everything that I was grateful for. So I started walking, and I thanked God for everything: my health, my strength, my right mind, that I can see, that I'm able to walk, the air, the scenery, the trees. The more I said, "Thank you," the taller I was standing. I felt like I had strength with each step. – *Shay*

God is my strength
So many people told me, "Be strong." What I learned is that it's okay to allow yourself to be weak, to allow yourself to be broken, and to ask God to be your strength. And He will. – *Marne*

Survivor Wisdom

Advice and encouragement from people who know the pain of loss.

QUESTION: What Bible Verses Have Helped You Make It Through?

Jeremiah 29:11 is my saving grace Scripture. "For I know the plans I have for you," declares the LORD, "plans to prosper you and not to harm you, plans to give you hope and a future." – *Krista*

I would think about Scriptures that are full of hope—remembering who I am in Christ, remembering that the enemy will tell me lies. – *Nicole*

Isaiah 41:10. I just held those words. When I was crying and sad, I was like, "You will never leave me. You will never forsake me. You are always faithful, and I know You will not leave me alone." – *Maria*

Even though I didn't want the separation or the divorce, I still had guilt. What did I do wrong? What could I have done? Acts 10:43 says, "Everyone who believes in him [Jesus] receives forgiveness of sins through his name." I thought about that a lot during the holidays. I knew I had forgiveness. – *Kathy*

Psalm 139 says that even the darkness was like light to God and that all the days in my life were ordained in God's book before even one of them came to be. I knew that even though this was dark to me, it wasn't dark to God. So if I could just hold on to God, He could lead me through what I needed to walk through. – *Monica*

Philippians 4:6 says, "Be anxious about nothing, and in everything by prayer and petition, give it to the Lord." And I do. It doesn't mean I don't have bad moments, but I can recover from them by going to the Bible, by picking up the phone with somebody I've met through church and those mentors I have in my life, and it passes. I know that's God, and I know He's there. – *Jan*

Are You Numbing Your Pain?

If you try to handle your pain by consistently numbing or avoiding it, the hurt will last longer and will be increasingly difficult to heal from.

Check the box of any descriptions that fit you:

- ☐ Working more and more hours because it helps me avoid feeling the pain.

- ☐ Engaging in sexual activity or a new relationship because it feels good to escape the emotional stress, and I long for human touch and a sense of desirability.

- ☐ Taking alcohol or drugs to temporarily numb the pain.

- ☐ Spending money on things I don't need because it momentarily feels good.

- ☐ Overactivity, such as church activities, holiday events, or volunteer work.

- ☐ Any increased behavior or action that I do because it helps me forget about my pain. (Note: The behavior itself might not be a wrong behavior, but the concern is when you are doing it too much in an effort to avoid your pain.)

"Sex, drugs, alcohol, or shopping can just add a layer of isolation to your life because you're not depending on God; you're not depending on others; and they don't give you anything to move forward. They add a layer of guilt and shame, and sometimes they'll add a layer of physical dependence. They help you dig the hole deeper," says Susan Lutz.

Sabrina Black offers this advice: "Sometimes that void is so large, you'll begin to fill it with other things if you don't fill it with God first. When you're feeling lonely, reach out in prayer or reach out for God's Word. Because there's that sense of emptiness right now, you want to make sure you fill it with an overwhelming presence of God."

If you have a void inside, you need to fill it with something. Choose wisely.

"Keep away from anything that might take God's place in your hearts." (1 John 5:21 NLT)

God, this is so hard. I can't do this alone. I can do this with You. Fill me with You—Your comfort and reassurance, Your wisdom and strength.

TAKEAWAY:
Be intentional about filling your void with good, godly things.

Allow Others to Help You

If you want to experience healing from the pain, and the accompanying sense of wholeness and peace, then you need the Lord and you need to allow Him to use other people to help you.

People want to help you and are able to help you, if you will allow them and offer some direction. "You were created for community; you weren't wired to do this by yourself," says Dr. Paul David Tripp, pastor and author.

How can others help? What can you ask of them? You'll want to be specific in communicating what would be helpful. Perhaps you need someone who has a truck to carry home the Christmas tree. Maybe you need someone to take your kids to a holiday event on an evening you need to work. Maybe you'd like a holiday invitation so you don't have to be alone on Christmas Day.

Jennifer shares how she asked for prayer the first Christmas after her divorce: "Be honest with friends and family and ask them to pray for you. I know the prayers held me up so many times during Christmas."

As you ask for prayer, let people know what they can pray for specifically, and not just that you will "make it through." Also ask them to pray that you will draw closer to the Lord and find deep, inner peace; that you'll be able to extend help and support to others this season; and that you'll experience a strength that you've never before had. Ask them to pray that you'll feel worthwhile and that you'll have the constant assurance you're not alone.

At times you'll still feel alone, even surrounded by supportive friends. Continue to turn to God. His presence is where wholeness and love are found.*

"Come near to God and he will come near to you." (James 4:8a)

You, Lord, are always with me. Give me the courage to ask for help and to receive it.

TAKEAWAY:

People want to help and are able to help, if you will allow them and offer some direction.

REFLECT:
List people God has put in your life who can help you.

What specific things can you ask of these people that would truly be helpful to you this holiday?

---

* See the article on page xiii to find out how God can become part of your life.

You're Never Alone

The holidays heighten feelings of loneliness. These steps are important in dealing with the pain of being alone:

1. Recognize that loneliness is what you're feeling.
2. Accept the reality of your situation.
3. Discover ways to help ease the lonely times.

"It was hard to see families around Christmastime. It magnified the fact that I was alone," shares Monica. "Normally, the feeling of loneliness comes and goes, but around Christmas I was more consumed with the fact that I'm by myself now."

While you might not be married anymore, you are never alone: "When you think about the fact that God is an ever-present help in times of trouble, that's a perfect time to just fall on your knees and cry out to the Lord and to experience the fact that He is Immanuel, 'God with you,'" says Sabrina Black.

Have you fallen on your knees before God, crying out to Him and giving Him everything that burdens you and threatens to engulf you? He is the all-sufficient God who loves you intensely, and He wants to show you the healing power of His presence.

"God is our refuge and strength, an ever-present help in trouble. Therefore we will not fear, though the earth give way and the mountains fall into the heart of the sea, though its waters roar and foam and the mountains quake with their surging. ... The LORD Almighty is with us; the God of Jacob is our fortress." (Psalm 46:1–3, 7)

REFLECT:
When are you loneliest?

How do you relate to Psalm 46 in today's reading?

God, You are the only one who truly knows the loneliness I'm struggling with. It feels like a hollow in my gut that often threatens to consume me. You are the only one who can remedy that. I need You to fill that emptiness. I want to know for sure that You are always with me and helping me through.

TAKEAWAY:
Just because you do not feel God's presence, does not mean He's not there.

Survival Tips

The charts, checklists, and exercises in this section will help you apply the practical ideas in this book to your own life.

Keep Yourself from Being Blindsided

Emotional ambushes are triggered by activities, traditions, songs, sights, sounds, etc., that remind you of past times. Mentally preparing yourself will help lessen the ambush factor.

"Going into that first holiday season, a number of things could catch you off guard. One thing you ought to do is replay in your own mind, well ahead of time, what the family traditions almost always involved so that you are expecting these things to happen." – Dr. Robert DeVries, counselor

Answer the questions below to help you think through potentially hard-hitting moments.

Holiday preparations

Your spouse likely had a certain role in decorating for the holidays, cooking/baking, gift-giving, etc. How will holiday preparations look different this year?

_____

_____

_____

_____

_____

Holiday get-togethers

How has your divorce affected whom you'll be getting together with this holiday season, compared to past holidays? (Will you miss seeing certain people; is there potential for awkwardness or discomfort; is there a possibility of conflict; etc.?)

_____

_____

_____

_____

Thanksgiving/Christmas Day

What will you miss most about your ex-spouse's presence on Thanksgiving/
Christmas Day?

_____

_____

_____

_____

If you and your ex-spouse will be splitting the time with your children, how will
that affect your holidays?

_____

_____

_____

_____

Holiday Journal:

What to Do with Your Holiday Emotions

A journal provides you an opportunity to face and deal with tough situations; it gives you a place to release pent-up emotions. It doesn't have to be neat, nor contain good grammar or spelling. Your journal is there as a healing tool, for your eyes only.

Use a separate notebook or journal to write your responses to one or more of the topics below.

☐ Psalm 147:3 says that Jesus heals the brokenhearted and binds up their wounds. Tell Jesus about why your heart is broken this holiday season, and ask Him to bind up your wounds.

☐ Read the comment below and share your personal thoughts about crying or showing emotions in public.

"Emotions are natural for all of us, and yes, other people may become uncomfortable with them, but they're genuine emotions. The Bible is filled with examples of people weeping in public. Crying is not shameful at all. A good show of emotion from time to time, even at a party, shows authenticity for the significant loss you've experienced in your life." – Dr. Robert DeVries

☐ Make a list of all the emotions you've been struggling with recently. (Optional: It's also very helpful to take each emotion separately and analyze it, by answering questions such as "What is this about? What exactly is triggering this emotion? What is at the heart of this issue?" Don't try to do this all in one sitting.)

CHAPTER 2:

Having a Plan

Planning gives you a degree of control over your emotions. And during times like these—when life has even more potential to feel out of control—deciding what you'll do and not do is wise.

This chapter discusses:

- Whether or not to continue holiday traditions that become difficult or uncomfortable without your spouse
- Why having a plan is crucial
- How to create a straightforward, yet flexible, plan
- How to take care of yourself and your children this season

Survivor Stories

Lesia and Linda realized that planning ahead would help minimize holiday stress and potential hurts.

"Because I knew it was going to be just me this Christmas, I started shopping back in August; I had it all done before Thanksgiving. I knew I had to plan because my finances were different. My mom and I planned how we were going to cook, and not a whole lot. That was a lot less stress. Christmas last year, when I was with my husband, was so tense. It is like night and day when I look at this Christmas and last Christmas." – *Lesia*

"It was Christmas Eve and my children's father picked them up for the weekend, but I had planned ahead. I did a bit of furniture arranging. I bought myself flowers. I bought myself what I wanted to eat. I bought a special piece of cake. I doled these out to myself all weekend. One thing you have to remember is that December 25th is just a day on the calendar. You can plan to celebrate Jesus' birthday with your children any day." – *Linda Ranson Jacobs, creator of DivorceCare for Kids*

The Strength to Survive

*These short daily readings will help you decide what to do
about your own holiday traditions and will help you
create a meaningful, doable, flexible plan that is suited to you.*

The Importance of Having a Plan

"Winging it is a poor choice if you're dealing with the holidays. Often it comes from, *I don't want to think about it; I don't want to deal with it*. But not thinking about it doesn't mean the holidays are going to disappear," says Dr. Susan Zonnebelt-Smeenge, psychologist.

As you approach the holidays, you will be faced with events, memories, traditions, expectations, and responsibilities. Having a plan keeps you from becoming overwhelmed.

Dr. Robert DeVries shares:

- Planning simply means that you decide what and how much you want to do.

- Prioritizing means that if there are 15 different activities you might be involved in over the holiday season, which one or two are most important to you?

Whatever you plan, be sure to allow yourself flexibility to adjust it. (And if you have children, invite them to help with the planning process; if they participate, the holidays may be more predictable and comforting to them.)

The thought of making a plan can seem daunting. You don't have to make your plan alone. Use the charts and tips in this book to guide you. Ask a family member or friend to help you make your plan. Be sure to invite God into your planning process.

"Good planning and hard work lead to prosperity, but hasty shortcuts lead to poverty." (Proverbs 21:5 NLT)

God, while my first inclination is to say, "I don't want to even think about planning for the holidays," I do want to get well, I do want to be able to face the holidays, and I want to move forward in healthy living. But I need Your help. Help me decide which activities to prioritize and which I can set aside, and grant me the courage and strength to follow through. I will listen for Your guidance.

TAKEAWAY:

Having a plan helps keep you from becoming overwhelmed.

Practical Ideas to Help You Plan

You can't do it all this holiday season. Whatever you think you must do, consider how you could simplify the plans that seem overwhelming or that may be a financial burden. (See the Survival Tips section at the end of this chapter to help you put your plan on paper.)

Look for a balance between meaningful and manageable.

Decorating: You don't have to put up every decoration. Consider which decorations are most important, in light of your circumstances and energy level. If you choose to have a tree, you do not need to use all the ornaments you normally would. Buy simple, colored bulbs instead. Decorate your tree with small stuffed animals instead of ornaments. Consider a tabletop tree or a meaningful centerpiece that focuses on the true meaning of Christmas. Use items from nature to decorate.

Shopping: Realize you don't need to purchase a gift for everyone this year. If finances are tight, consider a personal message in a card, a gift of a casserole, or a bag filled with that person's favorite snacks/treats. Be up-front with family and friends about changes in gift-giving. Also, to avoid a potentially stressful mall experience, shop online or from catalogs; these gifts can be sent directly to recipients.

Holiday cooking: Consider ways to simplify holiday meals: Have each guest bring a dish, lay out a simple buffet with turkey sandwiches and dressing, order out, go out, or ask someone else to plan this year's meal. You could skip cookie baking, or you could plan a cookie exchange at the office, where everyone brings a few batches of one type of cookie to share, so that everyone brings home a platter with a variety of cookies.

> **REFLECT:**
> *Which ideas in this article might work for you?*
>
> *Whom will you need to communicate these changes to?*
>
> *Reread Isaiah 58:9a and make that your prayer today.*

"Then you will call, and the LORD will answer; you will cry for help, and he will say: Here am I." (Isaiah 58:9a)

Lord, I need to make changes in my plans this year, but I don't want to let anyone down. Help me make wise decisions regarding holiday preparations. Please give me the courage to speak up and let others know I will be celebrating more simply this year and that I'd appreciate their support and understanding.

TAKEAWAY:

Consider beforehand what your holiday traditions/events might look and feel like without your ex. Having a realistic perspective helps protect you emotionally.

Holiday Traditions: Old vs. New

Many of your holiday traditions involved your former spouse. This year you'll need to decide which traditions you will keep (and how/whether to adapt them to your new situation), and you'll also have the opportunity to create new traditions.

"Creating new traditions is helpful because it gives me a way to celebrate what I do have instead of what I don't have," says Monica.

As you consider new traditions to develop, perhaps one of these ideas will interest you:

"I met another single mom. We talked on the phone and shared many meals. We began traditions together, such as making candied houses with our kids," says Jan.

"On Christmas Eve late at night, my children and I got hungry. We made pancakes, eggs, and bacon, and watched a Christmas movie. It's a new tradition," shares Monica.

"Christmas morning some of my family members went to an assisted living home and sang carols for the senior adults," says Mike.

"I bought two miniature Christmas trees to put in each child's bedroom for them to decorate however they wanted to," shares Linda. "They took the ornaments associated with their dad to put on their trees. It turned out to be very successful."

> **REFLECT:**
> In light of Monica's comment, "Creating new traditions is helpful because it gives me a way to celebrate what I do have instead of what I don't have," what do you have that you are thankful for?

As you plan new traditions, be careful not to discard every past tradition just because it is painful. "Some of the painful things in life are the most productive things in life," advises Dr. Paul David Tripp. "You don't want to back away from good, valuable traditions just because there is pain."

New traditions are good, but changing everything can also be overwhelming—especially if you have children (if you can, keep some old traditions for the benefit of your children). Try changing a few traditions and seeing which ones work and which ones don't. Traditions can be the source of bittersweet and even painful memories. But thankfully, you can create new traditions to anticipate and enjoy.

"Commit everything you do to the LORD. Trust him, and he will help you."
(Psalm 37:5 NLT)

God, I have good memories of holidays past, and I don't want to let go of that. But at the same time, it hurts to try and experience those same activities without my spouse. Please grant me the courage to try something new, and give me the strength to follow through on a past tradition that might be painful.

TAKEAWAY:

Consider beginning a new tradition this year, and decide which past traditions you'll maintain.

Laying the Foundation for Your Plan

As you make decisions about what activities to participate in, whom to spend time with, and how to handle unexpected situations, you'll want to lay the right foundation for your plans. Dr. Paul David Tripp describes three considerations:

Know yourself: Know your strengths and weaknesses. Make plans that focus on your strengths, and be cautious about those that might bring out your weaknesses. If spending time with your nieces and nephews brings you joy, plan a visit. If, at the office party, you might be tempted to numb your pain with alcohol or to find and connect with someone who finds you desirable— don't go. Put things on the calendar that will refresh your spirit: lunch with a same-sex Christian friend? An outdoor hike alone with God? A special church worship service or concert?

Know your family and friends: You have an idea of how family and friends will respond to you and what type of advice or support they'll give. Plan to spend time with those who will lift you up and encourage you in your faith. Plan to avoid those who will help fan the flame of negativity toward your ex-spouse or who will encourage you to lower your moral standards.

Know God: Know what God has promised to supply and deliver. "What has God said He will do for me in this particular moment?" Commit to reading and studying your Bible to find out (you can use online Bible study tools, ask your pastor or a Christian friend for guidance, or check if your Bible has a topical index or concordance). Not knowing what God promises sets you up to miss out on the help He offers, or to be disappointed because you're expecting God to do something He never said He'd do.

Building a foundation based on who you are and what God has promised will help ease your pain and keep you standing firm when you're considering unhealthy ways to escape. You'll also gain a greater awareness of God's faithfulness and provision in your life.

"The LORD is trustworthy in all he promises and faithful in all he does." (Psalm 145:13b)

God, You know me better than anyone, and You have promised to help me in all situations. Please help me to be prepared and strengthened for the coming days. You will never let me down. Thank You.

TAKEAWAY:

When you consider where to go and which people to spend time with, build your plan around who you are and what God has promised you in this situation.

Survivor Wisdom

Advice and encouragement from people who know the pain of loss.

QUESTION: How Do You Handle Gift-Giving on a Lower Budget?

I had to start preparing back in August or September and got a little bit at a time. Sometimes my daughter got the Nintendo game, sometimes she didn't. – *Thearon*

I'd make little coupon books: "This is good for an extra story at night" or "This is good for breakfast alone with Mom." – *Jan*

I was trying to make that first Christmas as close to normal as I could, meanwhile putting all that debt on my back. It was a big mistake. Things would have been better if I hadn't overspent that first Christmas. – *Kathy*

Every paycheck I put $20, $25 away. At the end of the year I split it by three and that's what my children get. – *Nicole*

How many gifts are under the tree is not nearly as important as whether I am spending the time with them to let them know they're a value to me. – *Laura Petherbridge*

This year two different small groups at our church adopted my children. My children were amazingly blessed with the gifts that they got. – *Susan*

A strategic way to ease the stress for your children over the holidays is to take them to a store, and it can be a dollar store, to help them pick out presents for their mom or dad or grandparent. – *Laura Petherbridge*

Often parents will try to make things up to their children by buying them new gym shoes or getting them a new bicycle, but that bicycle will turn into a car 10 years from now and they'll still be making you pay for that separation or divorce. Things happen in life and you cannot try to buy your way out of it. You need to help your children understand that "Our finances have changed, and all of us may need to make some sacrifices, and we will not increase our spending to make up for the difference." – *Sabrina Black*

When two parents who are divorced start trying to outdo the other by buying their kids' love or making themselves the favored parent, it often gets out of hand both for the parents and for the kids. Kids can see through that, and it's not really what they want anyway. They want to have a genuine relationship with you as their parent. – *Dr. Susan Zonnebelt-Smeenge*

If you have an ex who has the means to shower your children with gifts at the holidays and you cannot compete, that is really hard. If I were in that position, I would:

- Ask the Lord for a real heart where I could say to my children, "I'm glad you have a dad who loves you and has the means to give you this much for Christmas. I love you just like your dad does, but my money has to go further and my money has to cover a lot of the everyday things that we do just to keep our family going."

- Ask the Lord to give me ideas that don't cost money to reinforce the fact that I love them: like putting notes in their lunches or having ice cream for breakfast.

- Ask the Lord for the grace to help me figure out why I'm so upset about the other person's ability to give gifts that I can't give. Am I angry that he has more money than me? Am I sad that we're not doing it together? Am I fearful that my children's affections can be bought?

If you learn how to process those kinds of things with the Lord, you're less likely to have it impact your children or impact the way you deal with your ex.
– *Susan Lutz*

Take Care of Yourself

What have you been doing to take care of yourself this holiday season? Don't forget self-care in your holiday planning this year.

"It isn't healthy to expect yourself to be able to do all the things you used to do. Pacing yourself and having patience with yourself is so important," advises Dr. Susan Zonnebelt-Smeenge.

Emotional/mental health: Be sure that part of your holiday planning includes time for reflection, for processing the new emotions and stresses. As you face a holiday experience, an emotion, or a memory, write down what happened, how you reacted, how you feel about it now, and what you can learn from it. Use the Holiday Journal sections in this book to guide you in writing out your thoughts and emotions.

Physical health: The holidays will be easier to face if you get enough rest, get some exercise and sunlight, and eat wisely. "For me," shares Connie, "not getting enough rest made me vulnerable to not just being a weary griever, but also a depressed believer."

Spiritual health: Spiritual renewal and focus is a must. Only God can truly heal the pain and daily hurts that arise after a separation or divorce. "Open your Bible and meditate on the Word of God," says Sabrina Black. "The Twenty-third Psalm says, 'The Lord is.' Stop there and meditate on all the things the Lord is. Especially during your time of pain, the Lord is your comfort; the Lord is your keeper; the Lord is your safe place; the Lord is your refuge."

> **REFLECT:**
> In what ways this holiday season do you think you'll try to please other people (or do what they expect), possibly at your own expense?
>
> What action will you take to benefit your health?

"He [God] leads me beside quiet waters, he refreshes my soul. He guides me along the right paths." (Psalm 23:2b–3a)

God, sometimes I don't do a very good job of taking care of myself. I know what to do, but then I don't do it. Please strengthen me to make wise decisions about my body, my time, my emotional responses, and my spiritual focus. With You, I can do all things, and I can walk forward each day under Your protection.

TAKEAWAY:
Be intentional about self-care.

Help Your Children Through the Holidays

Your children might have concerns about the coming holidays. *How are we going to cut down the Christmas tree without Dad? Who is going to make our special Christmas breakfast without Mom here? If we aren't going to Grandma's for dinner, where will we go?*

They, too, will struggle with sadness, loneliness, and anger. In your holiday planning, make a point to think about …

1. How you'll prepare your children for the changes this season.

2. How you'll help them communicate and express their emotions.

Communicate changes in routines: Children find security in routines, explains Linda Ranson Jacobs, the creator of DivorceCare for Kids.* The holidays can send daily and weekly routines out the window. Let your children know ahead of time when and how plans will be changing, and remind them of differences in their usual routine.

Talk with them in advance: "I talked to my children before the holiday season started," shares Lois Rabey. "I said, 'We're going to do the best we can and celebrate what the season's about, even though Daddy's gone. We're going to have some new traditions, and it will be okay. There may be things you'll feel sad about. Come talk to me, and we'll work through it with God's help.'"

Include them in holiday planning: Include your children in the planning, says Dr. Robert DeVries. "We had a very hardy discussion among the three children and myself: Yes, we do want the tree; no, we don't have to put all the lights up outdoors; we're going to have our normal Christmas brunch, but we don't have to do Christmas cards."

Help them express their emotions: Your children, too, might be ambushed by emotions this holiday season. And when kids are upset about something, they often don't express their feelings in words. Instead, their fears and anxieties can come out in the form of misbehavior, throwing fits, or unusual quietness and withdrawal. Spend time working alongside or playing with your kids and open the door of communication by sharing what you're feeling (then make sure you listen instead of talk!). Consider introducing healthy emotional outlets such as clay sculpting, coloring, or water play, which can also be springboards for sharing.

Ask others for help and keep your family holiday plans simple. Encourage your children to talk to God about their hurts and worries. Let them know that with Jesus by their side, they can have peace, safety, and hope, even when they feel sad.

** To find out more about DivorceCare for Kids (DC4K) or to find a group for your kids, go to **dc4k.org**.*

"Don't worry about anything; instead, pray about everything. Tell God what you need, and thank him for all he has done. Then you will experience God's peace, which exceeds anything we can understand. His peace will guard your hearts and minds as you live in Christ Jesus." (Philippians 4:6–7 NLT)

Lord, taking care of my children is so difficult when I'm hurting this badly. Please give me a supernatural strength that will enable me to guide my children in healthy ways of coping and moving forward. I know I cannot be both mom and dad for my kids, so I will entrust my children to You, Heavenly Father. I pray that my children come to have a relationship with You.

TAKEAWAY:

Your children may be hurting too, and they need help in preparing for the changes and emotions of the holiday season.

Attending a DivorceCare support group will help you to know how to handle the tough emotions, what to expect in the days to come, how to take care of yourself, and where to find comfort. To find a group near you, go to **divorcecare.org** or call **800-489-7778**. Online groups are available!

Survival Tips

*The charts, checklists, and exercises in this section will help
you apply the practical ideas in this book to your own life.*

Be Careful Not to Overburden Yourself

"Think about what would make the holidays manageable and meaningful."
– Dr. Ramon Presson

Your energy is likely low this holiday season. It's wise to plan ahead and set
careful limits on what you're able to do this year. But be flexible. What you
decide today might change later, and that's okay.

Holiday decorations

1. Check the items below you'd like to do, those most important to you.
2. Describe how you might do them in a way that won't overburden you
   (see examples).

☐ Tree (e.g., get a smaller tree, buy a pre-decorated tree, have your
   nieces/nephews help you decorate, enlist help from a friend)

_____

_____

_____

_____

☐ Interior/exterior lights (e.g., only put lights inside this year, ask
   for help putting out exterior lights, use small electric candles
   in the windows instead)

_____

_____

_____

_____

☐ Other decorations

_____

_____

_____

_____

_____

_____

Christmas cards

Check what you might do this year. Only send cards if it is important/meaningful to you.

- ☐ Skip cards.

- ☐ Send a card or note via email or social media.

- ☐ Limit the number of cards you send (e.g., only to out-of-town relatives).

- ☐ Send a photo card of a beautiful scene, Scripture, or preprinted meaningful message.

- ☐ Ask someone to help you with cards:

_____

Gift-giving

Check ideas that will help keep gift-giving at a manageable level.

- ☐ Buy gift cards.

- ☐ Shop online or by catalog. Ask someone to help, if needed:

_____

- ☐ Shop early.

- ☐ Ask someone to go shopping with you—someone who will understand that this might be overwhelming for you.

- ☐ Brainstorm low-cost gift ideas, such as bags of assorted treats or framed photos.

- ☐ Give a gift to a cause in lieu of presents.

- ☐ Choose not to give gifts to everyone on your list, and prayerfully consider how to communicate that to family members.

Holiday Meals and Baking

Perhaps in the past you've done the bulk of the holiday meals and baking. Or maybe your former spouse was the person who spearheaded the holiday cooking. If you have children, you are probably hoping to keep things as "normal" as possible.

Be cautious this year about not overburdening yourself, and be sure to keep to your budget. Holiday meals can be meaningful and simple.

"My mom and I planned how we were going to cook, and not a whole lot. That was a lot less stress." – Lesia

Check ideas that might work for you this year.

- ☐ Allow someone else to host the Thanksgiving or Christmas meal.
- ☐ Have a potluck supper, where no one is responsible for the bulk of the cooking.
- ☐ Go out to a restaurant.
- ☐ Preorder a turkey/ham and side dishes.
- ☐ Choose not to make everything from scratch that you typically do.
- ☐ Enlist cleaning help for both before and after meals.
- ☐ Instead of inviting people for a large meal, have people for desserts and coffee instead.
- ☐ Buy cookies and/or desserts from the bakery or grocery store or use ready-to-bake cookies.
- ☐ Participate in a cookie exchange (where a group of friends each make four dozen of one type of cookie, and then everyone shares to create a variety platter to bring home).
- ☐ Other ideas:

  _____

  _____

  _____

  _____

  _____

  _____

When You Know
You'll Be Alone: Plan Ahead

Perhaps you are going to be without your kids or away from family this Thanksgiving or Christmas. How do you plan to take care of yourself during the time you won't have children or family around?

"Being alone during the holiday season is not the best position to be in. However, if you are going to be alone, it is helpful to map out a strategy to keep yourself on a positive, productive track." – Dr. Alfonza Fullwood, pastor

To start, try to make plans in advance to get together with someone. It could be a single-parent family, an elderly person without family nearby, a family from church, a same-sex neighbor or coworker who will be alone this holiday, friends from DivorceCare, or an international student or family.

But if you can't find anyone to spend time with, or you'd prefer to be alone, it's still important to plan your activities. Here are a few ideas of things you could do by yourself. Place a check next to those you'll plan to do!

☐ Get outdoors. Take a walk. Visit a beautiful local park or area and remember how God only makes perfect creations and He loves you perfectly. *Where I could go:*

_____

_____

_____

☐ Build something. Draw/write/sew/paint/create something. *What I could make:*

_____

_____

_____

☐ Buy or prepare a special treat to eat, something you don't get often or haven't had in a long time. Savor and appreciate it. *What I could get:*

_____

_____

_____

☐ Attend an event that's completely out of your normal habits: a live theater production, a classical concert, a school play, a talk or seminar, a sporting event, an open house. *My ideas:*

_____

_____

_____

- [ ] Serve someone in need (serve dinner at a shelter, give gifts to neighbors in need, visit a nursing home, etc.). *My ideas:*

  _____

  _____

  _____

  _____

- [ ] Investigate options and sign up for a class.

- [ ] Go to the gym and take a class or go swimming.

- [ ] Watch a movie or read a good book. *Movie and book ideas:*

  _____

  _____

  _____

  _____

- [ ] Schedule or give yourself a manicure or pedicure.

- [ ] Put together a jigsaw puzzle or a model plane/train/car/rocket.

- [ ] Plan a vacation or a tour of someplace new. Go online and look at ideas and options.

- [ ] Tackle a project you've been meaning to do for ages. It will feel so good to have it accomplished. *What I could do:*

  _____

  _____

  _____

  _____

- [ ] Read your Bible. Take extended time to pray for others. Write down God's promises and place them throughout your house.

- [ ] Schedule a massage or visit a local spa. Or plan an elaborate bubble bath at home with scents, bubbles, candles, and a cup of tea.

"Solitude can create opportunities for rest, for personal reflection, for spiritual growth, for productivity, getting things done, and also for creativity. What's crucial is that we don't allow solitude to become isolation, because isolation breeds loneliness and depression." – Dr. Ramon Presson

Holiday Journal:

Having a Plan

"We have a tendency to think of prayer as talking to God, a monologue. But if prayer is really a dialogue, after we express ourselves to God, we listen for what He might want to say to us. And I encourage people to do that by journaling."
– Dr. Ramon Presson

Be sure that part of your holiday planning includes time for reflection, for processing and talking with God about the emotions and stresses of the holidays. Use a separate notebook or journal to reflect on the topics below. Let this be a healing tool.

☐ The sights, sounds, and smells of the holiday season will trigger new waves of emotions and memories: Christmas lights in the neighborhood. Carols on the radio. Apple pie in the oven. Write about the sights, sounds, and smells that have been an emotional trigger for you. How did you react?

Holiday sights

_____

_____

_____

Sounds

_____

_____

_____

Smells

_____

_____

_____

☐ Lois Rabey encourages you to "lean in to the reality that God loves you." Describe how you've been leaning in to God and your struggles to do so. Write this in the form of a letter to God.

CHAPTER 3:

Tips for Surviving Social Events

You have to come to the party! It will be good for you, plus everyone will be excited to see you." So you go to the party with a plastic smile, cringe at people's "well-meaning" comments, hide out in the bathroom, and escape the party as soon as possible. Family get-togethers, office parties, yearly social events—all can be difficult for the person hurting from the pain of a marital breakup.

This chapter offers practical ideas on:

- Whether to attend the holiday event
- How to communicate your decision with the host
- How to handle awkward moments
- What to say to people who make hurtful comments
- What to do in the face of tears and emotional overload

Survivor Stories

Kathy felt like a fifth wheel at the annual party without her spouse. And Mike shares how a comment from a well-meaning relative triggered unwanted emotions at a social event.

"Some friends of ours always had a Christmas party, and we always went. After my husband left, I did go to the party once. It was awful. You're like a fifth wheel. I would walk up to one group and they would be talking about things they'd done together. What is there to talk about? What *I* did? Where *I* went? It was so uncomfortable. I would go to the bathroom. I would walk into the kitchen where the food was, hover in there for a while. I swore I would never go back to any more of those parties." – *Kathy*

"A family member brought up the fact that 'I guess this is your Christmas without your children.' I wish they hadn't said that, quite honestly. It brought tears to my eyes for a 10- or 15-minute period. I just nodded and said yes, and I didn't speak much because it was hard for me to speak." – *Mike*

The Strength to Survive

*These short daily readings will help you to find a healthy balance
between time spent alone and time spent with others, and to discover
how both can be helpful. You'll also find practical suggestions
on how to survive social events and how to deal with a bitter ex.*

Choosing to Spend
Time Alone or with Others

You may prefer surrounding yourself with people during the holidays, which
helps you forget your pain, or maybe you'd rather shut your doors and turn
out your lights, avoiding people altogether. To heal from your pain, you need
a healthy balance of privacy and interaction, and to experience the benefits of
each, it's important to evaluate situations before you are in them. Here are a
few questions to ask yourself before committing to a planned time of privacy
or interaction.

If I choose to be with people today, will I:

- Safely express my feelings if I am ambushed by difficult emotions?

- Be honest and ask for any needed help?

- Receive support as I seek to experience
  my pain and work through it?

If I choose to be alone, will I:

- Digest my latest feelings and thoughts?

- Talk to God about those feelings, seek His
  help, and accept His comfort?

- Avoid the temptation to numb my pain
  (drink excessively, take drugs, look at pornography, overeat, etc.)?

> **REFLECT:**
> *When you choose to
> be alone, what do you
> tend to do?*

If you would answer no to any of the above questions, rethink going into the
situation, or take steps to make the experience more beneficial. For instance,
if you tend to put on a mask and pretend you're okay with a certain friend,
consider telling your friend that you'd like to share the truth of your feelings
and that you could use a listening ear and prayers. If you realize that, when
alone, all you're going to do is gripe about your situation, consider choosing
to read a book on healing from the pain of separation and divorce instead.
The important thing is thinking before committing.

"[Jesus] went up on a mountainside by himself to pray. ... He was there alone."
(Matthew 14:23b)

REFLECT:
*Which suggestions will
you apply to help your
healing process?*

"Two are better than one. ... If either of them
falls down, one can help the other up." (Ecclesi-
astes 4:9–10a)

*God, even though my thoughts may be scattered
right now, give me the ability to think ahead
about the situations I'm going to be in. Help me
know what steps to take to allow both time with
others and time alone to contribute to my healing.*

TAKEAWAY:

Choose to spend time both alone and with others. Be intentional about making
those times healthy.

"I'd Rather Be by Myself"

The holidays can be exhausting, and sometimes it seems easier to just be by yourself. But too much isolation will make things harder for you. "When we isolate ourselves, we have one person to talk to usually—us," says grief therapist H. Norman Wright. "And since we're probably on a negative bent already, we're going to reinforce the negativism, and that's going to make it worse."

Sabrina Black agrees, "One of the biggest dangers in isolating yourself during the holidays is negative self-talk, feeling guilty about decisions that have been made and experiencing regret."

If your tendency is toward isolation, you might have already experienced some of the negative effects noted above. The solution is not to surround yourself with people; the answer lies in a healthy balance of both time alone and time with others—and more importantly, making wise choices regarding what you do when you're alone, the kind of people you're choosing to spend time with, and whether you are turning to God for help.

If time alone has resulted in negative self-talk, it doesn't always have to be that way. You can choose to reject those thoughts and believe what the Bible says about your situation. You can find Bible truths to fill your mind with in this book, use a Bible app to search for verses on various topics, or ask a Christian friend for help in searching the Scriptures.

"Finally, brothers and sisters, whatever is true, whatever is noble, whatever is right, whatever is pure, whatever is lovely, whatever is admirable … think about such things." (Philippians 4:8)

God, I sure do know what negative self-talk is. When I'm alone, please help me focus on what is good, holy, and uplifting. Help me to remember that it's harmful and exhausting to sit around and let the negative seep in, and that it's healing and helpful to intentionally choose prayer, Bible reading, journaling, or uplifting music.

> **REFLECT:**
> *When negative self-talk starts in your mind, what should you do to counter those thoughts?*

TAKEAWAY:

You can encourage yourself or you can discourage yourself. It's your choice.*

---

* See the Survival Tips exercise on "Controlling Negative Self-Talk When You're Alone" at the end of this chapter.

Survivor Wisdom

Advice and encouragement from people who know the pain of loss.

QUESTION: What Kind of People Should You Spend Time with This Holiday?

It's important to identify who are the safe people in your life. Who are the ones who are going to nurture you, to build you up? Not to berate you or say, "Well, get over it. You know it's been six months now." – *H. Norman Wright*

Try hard not to get in that circle of friends who lean toward vices you know are going to be detrimental to your recovery. – *Dr. Alfonza Fullwood*

You know the ones who are safe to spend time with and those who always pull you down. – *Sabrina Black*

You want somebody who knows that ultimately your healing is not going to come from within yourself. Your healing is going to come when you learn to bring all your pain and loss to the Lord. That person will kindly but persistently encourage you in that direction. – *Susan Lutz*

It was hard to make it through with no family around, so I made some phone calls and tried to get closer to the people at church; I felt like they were part of my family. – *Bill*

Church can be one of the places that's the most difficult to go to, but church is also the place you're going to receive the most help and care. – *Lois Rabey*

You want somebody who's not afraid of suffering, somebody who knows you'll get through on the other side and who is ready to walk with you and wait with you as that process continues. – *Susan Lutz*

Make sure you're around some other people who understand the same pain that you're going through. – *Laura Petherbridge*

When I've had such desperate feelings of loneliness, especially at the holidays, it's been important for me to see how other folks have felt the same way and to be told, "Hang on; it feels like you might not make it, but you are going to make it." – *JoAnne*

Survivor Wisdom

Advice and encouragement from people who know the pain of loss.

QUESTION: Should You Attend That Event or Not?

Don't commit to that party just because you want to please someone.
– *Dr. Zoricelis Davila*

Sometimes it helps to find out, who else is going to be at this gathering? Are these people you feel comfortable with, that you want to spend some time with? Or are they people where, "I don't know if I want to be around them this year"? This could be family. – *H. Norman Wright*

The person who is hurting tends to look for things to numb that pain. So don't expose yourself. Stay away from those things. – *Dr. Alfonza Fullwood*

You don't have to do it all. Picking one or two holiday events and trying to make yourself get through those is all you need to do. You can take that responsibility and make it through. – *Dr. Susan Zonnebelt-Smeenge*

If you don't feel up to it, let your host know you're not able to make it. Thank your host for the invitation, and encourage him or her to invite you again. You need to do what's best for you in this hour. – *Sabrina Black*

You might have to learn to be assertive because you might say to people: "I can only come for an hour."
"Oh no, no, you need to come for the whole time."
"Thank you for the invite, but I will be able to come for an hour."
And you repeat that two or three times in a very gentle, loving way.
– *H. Norman Wright*

I challenge people not to do the "all or nothing." What is healthy for each of us is to try to do "something." I'd say, "I'm going to go with the goal, first, of just staying a half an hour. And if I make it, I can leave." – *Dr. Susan Zonnebelt-Smeenge*

"I Don't Want to Bring Others Down"

"I didn't want to be the dark cloud over the celebration. So I put on a happy face and tried to be the sister, the daughter, the aunt that everybody wanted to see. Putting on that happy face was a heavier burden than I was emotionally able to carry at the time," shares Mardie.

Pretending you are doing fine not only hurts you, but is unfair to those around you. "Other people have different expectations then," says Dr. Susan Zonnebelt-Smeenge. "They expect that you're doing well and that you won't need any more from them. You're sabotaging yourself if you aren't honest."

Think about times you've said, "I'm doing okay," when inside you were screaming the opposite. Are there certain people you pretend with? How does it hurt you (and others around you) when you are not honest about your healing?

H. Norman Wright offers this advice: "You could be at a holiday gathering and all of a sudden the tears come. Best thing is, let them come, and don't apologize. Take charge of it and say, 'I'm crying because I've experienced a devastating loss.' That's all you have to say."

REFLECT:
Name the people you typically pretend around, saying "I'm okay" when you're not.

What holds you back from being honest around those people?

A marital breakup can be devastating. The fact that you might not be feeling holiday cheer is normal. Let others know you are going to be honest with them, and let them know what to expect from you this holiday season. Your honesty sets a precedent for future times when family or friends might be experiencing a personal struggle themselves, and you'd want them to be truthful with you.

"Therefore each of you must put off falsehood and speak truthfully to your neighbor, for we are all members of one body." (Ephesians 4:25)

Lord, I admit I've put on that happy-face mask. Help me to be honest with others so I can move forward and not backward in my healing process. Give me the humility to accept help, support, and prayers from others.

TAKEAWAY:
It is okay to admit you are hurting, even when others think you shouldn't be.

Handling Awkward Comments and Prying Questions

At social events and get-togethers, people sometimes don't know what to say to you and often will say the wrong thing. "I had a friend say to me on Christmas Day, 'This must be really hard for you to be single and watch your children have Christmas without their dad,'" shares Susan, "and then she elaborated and went into way too much detail about the things that my children were missing and about how lonely I must be."

Other times people ask prying, inappropriate questions that make you uncomfortable. "The best thing is to take charge of the moment and say, 'I would appreciate you not asking that question,'" advises H. Norman Wright. "If they continue, say the same thing word for word, and you'll take control of that situation. Trying to dance around the question is just going to encourage the individual. It's best to stop the line of questioning right up front."

Most of the time, people are not asking questions with the intent to hurt you or to bring you down. "Understand they may just be making conversation," explains Elsa Kok Colopy. "Sometimes understanding there's not a malicious intent in their asking can help settle the feelings that might come up in response."

While some people may continue to say the wrong things or act in ways that are hurtful, please remember that Jesus came to heal the brokenhearted. He came to heal you. Turn to Him with your hurts and feelings of vulnerability.

"LORD, you know the hopes of the helpless. Surely you will hear their cries and comfort them. You will bring justice to the orphans and the oppressed, so mere people can no longer terrify them." (Psalm 10:17–18 NLT)

Lord, You always know the right thing to say to me. What an amazing relief to be able to share my thoughts, fears, worries, and sadness with You, without judgment and without hurtful remarks. You are always faithful to comfort me in my pain.

REFLECT:
If a well-meaning friend says something hurtful or prying at the party, what response could you say to graciously close the conversation?

TAKEAWAY:

People will say hurtful things and ask inappropriate questions, but you can handle that in a way that's kind but firm.

Dealing with a Bitter Ex

During the holidays you might come into more contact with your former spouse than usual. When your relationship with your ex is bitter or hostile, you have choices on how to handle this relationship over the holiday season.

In all situations, do everything within your ability to decrease the tension. This might involve lessening interactions with your ex; keeping your words, body language, and actions humble and in check; and communicating ahead of time with him or her.

Pray before the interaction: "If you know you're going to have an encounter with the person you're no longer married to during the holiday season, that's the perfect opportunity to call on God," says Sabrina Black. "You don't want to get baited into an argument, so pray before you go and ask the Lord that you would be able to speak with kindness."

Choose not to let your ex's responses control you: Decrease your own tension by reminding yourself that your ex's behavior, feelings, and words are not yours to control and his or her responses shouldn't control you. "In your heart and mind give your ex permission to be angry and upset [this doesn't mean you agree with the behavior, but you realize it's your ex's choice, not yours], and tell yourself, 'I wish it weren't this way, but it is. It doesn't have to cause me to respond in the same way,'" suggests H. Norman Wright.

Communicate holiday plans in advance: If possible, communicating with your former spouse about holiday plans can help, and if you have children, it is necessary. In a volatile situation, keep conversations regarding children short and to the point. The holiday season will be taking its toll on all of you, so be careful to avoid making loaded comments or rolling your eyes in frustration, which only makes things worse for everyone.

"Be completely humble and gentle; be patient, bearing with one another in love." (Ephesians 4:2)

God, I have the choice to face my ex-spouse with godliness and humility, and I can choose responses that are good and right with You by my side. Help me to speak and act with kindness.

TAKEAWAY:
You can be proactive in lessening the tension when interacting with a bitter ex.

Survival Tips

The charts, checklists, and exercises in this section will help you apply the practical ideas in this book to your own life.

Social Event Survival

Preparation is key! These ideas can help make it easier for you to attend holiday and social events. Check the ideas that you might implement.

- ☐ Arrive late and/or leave early.

- ☐ Communicate any concerns ahead of time with the host; for instance, don't try to set me up with anyone, don't press me to drink alcohol, don't feel bad if I'm not upbeat, let me be me.

- ☐ Beforehand, ask people to pray for you while you're at the event. *Someone I can ask:* _____

- ☐ Remember that you might see people who aren't aware of the breakup and who might ask where your spouse is, then press for details. If people are asking you questions you don't want to answer, Dr. Ramon Presson offers this counsel:

    "You don't have to talk about your divorce if you don't want to. It's not being impolite to say, 'I really appreciate your concern, but I'd rather not talk about it right now.' Then you change the subject by shifting the focus onto them by asking a question about something they would be interested in."

- ☐ Sit in the back row or by the door, if applicable. Attend with someone who will understand when you're ready to leave. *Someone who could come with me:* _____

- ☐ Have someone you can call if you are attending the event alone and it becomes too much. *Someone I can call:* _____

- ☐ Identify a place ahead of time where you can go for a while if you're emotionally overwhelmed. *Places I can retreat to in the home or building:* _____

- ☐ Go with an advocate—someone who will help you interact with (or graciously put in line) people who might push you to get together with someone of the opposite sex, pressure you to indulge in alcohol, want to bad-mouth your spouse (that's not helpful to you), tell you things you don't want to hear, etc. *Someone to be my advocate:*

_____

What to Say When ...

You're invited to a party. You plan to attend, but have misgivings. People's questions and comments can be prying and exhausting.

Use these responses to help communicate with the host before you attend and with people at the party.

1. Send the responses to people in advance (you might combine more than one). Be sure to be gracious and appreciative of the invitation.

2. Write responses on an electronic device or paper for your own reference.

Only for a Few Hours Thanks for the invite. I do plan to attend, but I'll only be able to stay for a few hours. If on that day I feel like staying longer, is it okay if I let you know then?	***I Might Change My Mind*** Yes, I plan to attend. Please be aware I might change my mind or I might need to leave early. Do not feel bad or take it personally.
Changing the Topic Thank you for asking. I'm working on that with God's help ... But tell me instead about [shift conversation to a topic of interest to that person].	***I'm Not Ready*** Thank you for the invitation, but I'm not ready this year to spend several hours with others celebrating. Be sure to ask me again next year.
Don't Set Me Up with Anyone I know you want what you think is best for me, but please don't try to set me up with anyone. It's important for me to focus on my healing and my spiritual and emotional health right now.	***Not Having Alcohol*** I'll just be having soda and water. While numbing my stress and pain is tempting, it's wiser for me to keep my head clear and make choices that are ultimately for my own good.
Bashing My Ex Isn't Helpful When people make negative comments about my ex, it's not helpful to me. Please help me keep my focus on things that are uplifting and good in my life.	***Don't Worry If I Cry*** Please be aware that I might start crying, and that's okay. Tears are part of my healing process, and it's important that I allow myself to grieve what I've lost.
Help Me Stay Positive Sometimes people make negative comments about my ex in an attempt to be "supportive" of me. I want to be careful not to plant any more seeds of bitterness inside myself than I already have. Please help me in this.	***Would Rather Not Talk About It*** I appreciate your concern, but I would rather not talk about it right now ... So tell me what's new in your life [or, tell me how your parents/children/etc. are doing; tell me how your job is going].
Your Prayers Are Welcome I know you mean well in your comments, but what I ask is that you pray for this situation.	***What's Helpful*** Please don't try to cheer me up or offer advice. A hug, your presence, your support and affirmation are all I need. I appreciate your love and care.

Controlling Negative Self-Talk
When You're Alone

Spending time alone during the holidays can be productive, but a danger to avoid and prepare for is negative self-talk when you're alone.

I can't do this on my own. It's all my fault. No one understands. I must not be worth it. No one truly cares. I'll show my ex! There's nothing left to live for. The loneliness is overtaking me. If only I …

To control negative self-talk, you have to counter it with God's truth. These examples from Carla and Nicole will show you how:

Negative self-talk: *"No one can relate to this. I'm really alone in this." – Carla*

> **CHARACTERISTICS OF NEGATIVE SELF-TALK:**
> *It's not true.*
>
> *It does not build you up or help you grow.*
>
> *It exaggerates the impact.*

If I feel alone this holiday, the truth is: God says He is with me, and He has given me people in my life who care for me. "The LORD is close to the brokenhearted." (Psalm 34:18a) "Finally, brothers and sisters … encourage one another … and the God of love and peace will be with you." (2 Corinthians 13:11) *"The truth is, God can equip other people to care for us." – Carla*

Negative self-talk: *"I felt a heavy weight of sadness, hopelessness, thinking, 'I'm going to live the rest of my life sad.'" – Nicole*

If I feel the sadness will never end, the truth is: God has a plan and purpose for my life. He knows what the future holds for me, and He promises it is good. "'For I know the plans I have for you,' declares the LORD, 'plans to prosper you and not to harm you, plans to give you hope and a future.'" (Jeremiah 29:11) *"I know I'm going to be restored. And there's nothing I'm going through, no pain I'm going through, that He hasn't already gone through and conquered." – Nicole*

In your life

What negative self-talk goes through your mind when you don't rein it in?

_____

Prayerfully write down a truth from God that you've learned.

_____

_____

_____

Holiday Journal:

Tips for Surviving Social Events

Writing out thoughts and feelings, hurts and frustrations, helps you make sense of your feelings. Write your responses to one or more of the topics below in a separate notebook or journal. Or you could choose to write about a different topic.

- ☐ What concerns do you have about attending the different events and get-togethers coming up this season? (You could address each event separately.)

- ☐ How do you feel about attending church during the holidays?

- ☐ List the safe, uplifting people in your life you'll want to make a point to spend time with this holiday. Describe why you chose each of these people.

- ☐ Explain what has been the most difficult part of the holidays so far.

CHAPTER 4:

Surviving Thanksgiving and Christmas Day

W hen you were a child, you likely looked forward to Thanksgiving and Christmas Day, anticipating the gifts, the turkey and dressing, the sugar cookies, the colored lights, and the family traditions. Then when you were married, you and your spouse created new holiday traditions that you looked forward to just as much.

This year, everything has changed. With a feeling of dread, you might wonder, *Just how hard is that day going to be? And what happens beyond that day?* This chapter discusses:

- How looking outside yourself to others helps you

- What the Bible says about reconciliation

- Whether or not it gets any easier

- How you can have hope

Survivor Stories

Monica hadn't expected Christmas Day to be so draining. And Bill was unprepared to deal with his daughter's emotions on Christmas Eve.

"Christmas Day was horrible. I didn't want my kids to have to split the day with Mom or Dad, so we decided my husband would come over to our house. He came in, and I was filled with such a feeling of loss that I had to run to the other room and cry. I cried all day. I would close the door, lock myself in the bathroom for a little while, get my composure back, and then go back out and try to be with my kids in a happy way. It was draining, very draining." – *Monica*

"On Christmas Eve, I went to church, came back, and sat down to have dinner with my son and my daughter. My daughter was very disturbed because she knew what was going on: *Mom wasn't home.* I said, 'We're going to make it through this. Daddy's here. Daddy's not going to leave you guys alone.' And she started answering me back and was aggressive toward us, and then she rushed from the table and left up to her room." – *Bill*

The Strength to Survive

These short daily readings will help you find a reason for hope in the face of sadness and despair over the breakup of your marriage.

Help Others Who Might Need You

Consider spending Thanksgiving, Christmas, or New Year's with someone who is alone this holiday season: It could be someone who's experienced a loss, someone without family nearby, or a nursing home resident. If God puts the thought of a certain person on your heart, don't immediately dismiss that person because you don't think he or she would be interested. Take a chance. You may be pleasantly surprised.*

You could also volunteer to help serve a holiday meal at a shelter, hospital, Salvation Army, fire or rescue station, or church. Find available opportunities in your community. Other ideas would be delivering cards or cookies to someone who is hurting or lonely, or making encouraging phone calls.

"This year my children and I had Christmas Eve day together. Instead of doing things for ourselves, we decided to go to a shelter and help out. We prepared meals and toys. The three of us spent hours there and had a blast giving back to somebody else who was less privileged. My children said, 'Let's do that for Christmas next year,'" shares Christina.

"Praise be to the God and Father of our Lord Jesus Christ, the Father of compassion and the God of all comfort, who comforts us in all our troubles, so that we can comfort those in any trouble with the comfort we ourselves receive from God. For just as we share abundantly in the sufferings of Christ, so also our comfort abounds through Christ." (2 Corinthians 1:3–5)

God, who needs my help and support? Who is hurting or alone or in need? Help me look at those around me with new eyes. Help me give Your comfort to someone else this holiday season. So many people are hurting, and many pretend everything is fine. Lead me to them. And give me the courage and energy to follow through.

> **REFLECT:**
> What does
> 2 Corinthians 1:3–5
> say about comfort?

TAKEAWAY:
Helping others eases your pain.

* Always remember that inviting a person of the opposite sex is not wise if you are recently divorced or if your divorce is not final. A new relationship might be the last thing on your mind, but understand the other person might think differently. Your healing is of utmost importance, so do not jeopardize that.

Hoping for Reconciliation

"In the back of my head the entire time of Christmas was, *My husband is going to come back to me. He's waiting for a special occasion*," shares Jennifer. "*He's going to come back with this big ring; he'll show up and beg me for forgiveness.* Christmas came and went, and I didn't even hear from him."

Your greatest wish and prayer may be for the reconciliation of your marriage, and reconciliation is a wonderful, godly choice for a marriage. But it's not always possible. Dr. Paul David Tripp shares sage advice for those hoping for reconciliation this holiday season:

- God is a God of restoration, and you should want peace; you should want reconciliation. Those are good things to desire. They're not good things to demand.

- Keep your standards high. Don't be willing to lower your standards in order to create reconciliation. What you're doing then is you're building a house on a bad foundation, and it's going to come down.

- Reconciliation is an [agreement] between two people. You can't make reconciliation happen yourself, so you must be realistic about whether your ex shares this desire.

- You don't reconcile by making bargains. You reconcile by two people being committed to God's standards. You never reconcile by saying, "If you do this, I'll do that." You will always regret those kinds of bargains.

By all means pray for reconciliation and take steps forward in spiritual growth to prepare for that possibility. These actions draw you closer to God, which strengthens and empowers you to face whatever the future may bring. Accept the fact that God doesn't promise to restore all broken marriages. He has promised to renew all individuals who turn to Him. And He can use your worst circumstances to bring about that transformation.

"The LORD will guide you always; he will satisfy your needs in a sun-scorched land and will strengthen your frame. You will be like a well-watered garden, like a spring whose waters never fail." (Isaiah 58:11)

Lord, I pray for the reconciliation of my marriage, but according to Your terms, not mine or my former spouse's. If it's not possible, help me accept that You are all I need. I can be healed, whole, peaceful, and joyful with You by my side.

TAKEAWAY:
Reconciliation should be on God's terms, not your spouse's or yours.

What Are You Focusing On This Christmas?

"It's important to remember that the holiday wasn't created simply for the relationship you had with your [ex-spouse], but that the holiday itself has a meaning that goes far deeper than any one relationship might have gone," explains Dr. Robert DeVries.

So what is the true meaning of Christmas?

"The true meaning of Christmas is about what God has done—that God has come near to us in Christ," says Dr. Alfonza Fullwood. "Christmas is about Christ. Christmas is a source of hope for those who are suffering, because Christmas reminds me that God loves me. He cares for me. He's near me. He's come to me in His Son."

Consider what we are celebrating at Christmas. It will give you a new perspective on your situation.

REFLECT:
Turn to pages xiii–xv in this book. Prayerfully read the article and listen for what God is saying to you through His words and promises.

Christ came to save us from our sin. He is with us always: "And she [Mary] will have a son, and you are to name him Jesus, for he will save his people from their sins … and they will call him Immanuel, which means 'God is with us.'" (Matthew 1:21–23 NLT)

God loves us so much. He sent His Son to save us from sin and give us eternal life: "For God so loved the world that he gave his one and only Son, that whoever believes in him shall not perish but have eternal life. For God did not send his Son into the world to condemn the world, but to save the world through him." (John 3:16–17)

Lord and Savior, You came to earth to save us and set us free from the worst darkness of all. Your birth is about hope, forgiveness, freedom, salvation, and most of all love. Help me to turn my focus to You, to consistently draw near to You, and to receive the gifts You are giving me.

TAKEAWAY:

Christmas is about Christ's coming to save the world from sin and suffering.

The Basis for Hope

"When you've experienced a deep loss, it tends to dominate your life.

> You feel despair, but Jesus came to give you hope.
> You feel sadness, but Jesus came to bring joy into your life.
> Your life is in turmoil, yet Jesus came to bring peace to your life.
> Much of your time is dominated by tears,
> > but Jesus came to wipe away every tear.

"He is your source of strength, and He is your stability." – *H. Norman Wright*

The Bible describes God's plan to remove suffering and provide us with lasting comfort and eternal life. To understand it, we need to see why we suffer in the first place. We suffer for many reasons: because we live in a world of sickness and disaster, because of the evil actions of others, and because of the consequences of our own disobedience to God (the Bible calls this "sin"). God is pure and holy: He cannot tolerate sin. Not only does our sin keep us from God, it also has consequences—suffering in this life and physical death followed by eternal punishment.

So, where is the hope? God loves us so much and does not want us to suffer. He has provided a way to release us from the penalty and presence of sin, both now and eternally. He sent His Son, Jesus Christ (who was sin-free), to be born on this earth and pay the penalty for our sins. Through Jesus, our sins are forgiven and our slate is wiped clean. And one day He will remove all sin and suffering from the world. This is reason for great hope.*

"When God our Savior revealed his kindness and love, he saved us, not because of the righteous things we had done, but because of his mercy. He washed away our sins, giving us a new birth and new life. … Because of his grace he declared us righteous and gave us confidence that we will inherit eternal life." (Titus 3:4–5, 7 NLT)

Faithful God, I can trust You. You have a plan to take care of me, if I will turn my life over to You. Through You, we have the promise of everlasting life in an amazing place called heaven, a place that is just as real as the air I breathe.

TAKEAWAY:
God provides you with real hope amid your grief.

---

* To learn more about God's gift of hope and forgiveness, read the article "What to Do with Guilt and Regrets" on pages xiii–xv.

Reflect On What You've Learned

When the holiday season comes to a close this year, we encourage you to take inventory of these past several weeks.

- What was the most difficult part of the holidays? What ideas did you implement that worked well? What didn't work or was stressful?

- What have you learned about yourself? What have you learned about God?

Spending time in reflection will help you heal from your hurts. We recommend you write down your responses to these questions; this is more effective than just thinking about them. (See this week's Holiday Journal on page 62.)

H. Norman Wright talks about how, as you reflect on your situation, you might be tempted to focus only on the negative, or to stuff the hurt and look only at the good:

"Some people focus more on the pain and the hurt, and that's very, very normal. Eventually, we look at the hurt, but [our cry] turns into: *Here is where I am. What can I learn through this? How can I grow? What are the blessings I have experienced in spite of the depth of my pain?*

"Then there are other people who focus on the blessings, and they deny the hurt. It's important that we work toward the place where we can talk about the pain, but at the same time: *Here's what I've learned about God. Here's where He has been present for me.*"

For some people, a time of reflection can turn into a rehashing of what they wish they'd done differently and what they did or didn't do that may have contributed to the breakup.

If you find your reflection process is turning more into a litany of regrets, remember that everyone who believes in Jesus is credited with His righteousness—with His perfect standing in God's eyes. So if you're trusting in Christ as Lord of your life, in a real sense, God considers you to be a perfect person. That's why He accepts you. Even though God knows He's still working on you.*

"I remember my affliction and my wandering, the bitterness and the gall. … Yet this I call to mind and therefore I have hope: Because of the LORD's great love we are not consumed, for his compassions never fail. They are new every morning; great is your faithfulness." (Lamentations 3:19, 21–23)

Lord, I've learned some tough lessons, and I know there's more to learn. But instead of feeling down about my situation, help me to have a clear vision of how You're growing and shaping me into an instrument of Your peace and love.

TAKEAWAY:
Reflect on the good lessons you are learning.

* To find out how this applies to you, read "What to Do with Guilt and Regrets" on page xiii.

Looking Beyond the Holidays

"Finally, brothers and sisters … encourage one another … and the God of love and peace will be with you." (2 Corinthians 13:11)

The holidays are coming to an end, and the new year is approaching. As you continue to walk through the grieving process, you will need help and encouragement. The Bible says we were created to be in relationship with other people: to interact with, care for, encourage, and support. God wants us to accept help from other people.

"Healing from trauma or grief happens in the context of community. I don't know of any other way of finding healing that is not in the context of finding others who can help you," says counselor David Bueno Martin.

REFLECT:
Who are the safe people in your life? Those who will not judge, but will pray with you, cry with you, and point you to the Lord for help?

If you do not have people in your life who encourage you and point you toward God's help and healing, pray that God will lead you to safe, uplifting people who will walk alongside you on your journey.*

"You have seen my troubles, and you care about the anguish of my soul. You have … set me in a safe place." (Psalm 31:7b–8 NLT)

Lord, please guide me to people who will support and uplift me through my journey of grief and healing. Give me the courage to take the step of reaching out to people for help. And thank You for the safety of Your presence and Your promises.

TAKEAWAY:

Make a point to be with people who will support and care for you as you recover from your separation or divorce.

* DivorceCare is a safe place where others have an idea of what you are facing and want to help.

To find a DivorceCare support group near you, go to **divorcecare.org** or call **800-489-7778**. Online groups are meeting too.

Survival Tips

The charts, checklists, and exercises in this section will help you apply the practical ideas in this book to your own life.

Be Thankful

Thankfulness is a healing tool. There's always something to be thankful for:

"I'm grateful to have my family." – Shay

"I'm thankful that I have my basic needs met. I'm grateful just for the breath of life." – Krista

"I'm grateful that Christ came into my life because I can't imagine my life without Him. It's very hopeful to know that I'm not alone." – Krista

"I appreciate God's forgiveness because I know I can stand before God righteous. I thank God for the gift of my salvation." – Nicole

What are you thankful for?

Circle what you are thankful for.

The support of my family.

My children.

My health.

That I have a job.

How God is helping me, comforting me, and providing for me in my pain.

My church.

My friends.

Good memories.

God and His promises.

My DivorceCare group.

Write down anything else that you are thankful for today.

_____

_____

_____

_____

_____

Helping Others Helps You

A way to ease your loneliness and pain is to focus on helping others. There are so many opportunities for you to help others.

"One way you can shift your focus off of the pain is to focus on helping other people while you are hurting." – Dr. Alfonza Fullwood

Do not be overwhelmed by this list. Carefully read the ideas, and mark any that might suit you. These ideas are just to help you broaden your thinking of areas where you could help. Pick one thing and then do it.

Call, visit, invite over, or bring a gift to:

- ☐ An elderly friend/homebound person
- ☐ Someone with no family in the area
- ☐ An exchange student/international university student
- ☐ A single-parent family or a single parent alone this holiday
- ☐ Someone grieving a loved one's death
- ☐ Someone facing a separation or divorce or marital problems
- ☐ A family or child in financial need
- ☐ Someone who has comforted you
- ☐ Other idea:

_____

Help a family, friend, or group with a physical/practical need

- ☐ Staying with an ill loved one to provide a break for the caregiver
- ☐ Child care, especially for a single parent
- ☐ Gardening/yard work
- ☐ Painting/repairs
- ☐ Housework
- ☐ Meals
- ☐ Other idea, suited to your skills/strengths:

_____

Serve others in need through a local organization

- ☐ Nursing home/assisted living facility
- ☐ Soup kitchen
- ☐ Salvation Army

- ☐ Women's shelter/pregnancy center
- ☐ Jail/prison
- ☐ Detention home
- ☐ Volunteering at a walk/run for a cause
- ☐ Church ministry
- ☐ Library/community organization

Serve holiday dinner or bring homemade treats to those who serve your community

- ☐ Fire department
- ☐ Rescue squad
- ☐ Hospital workers

Pray that God will bring to mind someone who needs your words, your hands, your prayers this season. Your church pastor will also have suggestions of people who are alone this holiday season and places to volunteer.

Make a list of people and their needs, and pray for them

- ☐ _____
- ☐ _____
- ☐ _____
- ☐ _____
- ☐ _____

"Serve one another humbly in love." (Galatians 5:13b)

Holiday Journal:

Surviving Thanksgiving and Christmas Day

Use a separate notebook or journal to write out your responses to one or more of the topics below.

☐ Describe what this year's Thanksgiving/Christmas Day will look like without your ex-spouse. Will it be better or worse? Why?

☐ Write a response to God in light of the fact that He is with us. Share your thoughts honestly with God, and take time to listen for what He wants to say to you.

"One of the main messages of Christmas is that God not only exists, but He leans in, He cares, and He's involved. Our God is not a distant, detached observer, but God in Christ Jesus, Immanuel, is with us, and He is for us. We're not alone." – Dr. Ramon Presson

☐ Christ is coming again to join with Him all who've given their hearts to Him—those both in heaven and on earth. Express in your journal what you are thankful for regarding Christ's coming.

Take Inventory

When the holiday season comes to a close this year, we encourage you to take inventory of these past several weeks.

What ideas did you implement that worked well?

_____

_____

What didn't work or was stressful?

_____

What do you think you'll do differently next year?

_____

_____

List the three most important ideas you've learned from the Surviving the Holidays program.

_____

_____

If You Feel Suicidal

Thoughts of wanting to escape the pain are normal, and you may even have thought you cannot live without your former spouse. If you have considered taking your life or have considered how you would plan to do that—pick up the phone.

"Many times individuals have thoughts of, *I just don't want to live anymore*," says H. Norman Wright, an expert in crisis counseling and intervention. *"Anytime you have a pattern of suicidal thinking, let somebody else know, because the main problem right now is that the only person you're talking with is yourself, and you're not getting good advice from yourself.* Find somebody you trust. It could be a pastor, a counselor, a good friend who is going to listen to you.

"Realize that fleeting thoughts like this are quite normal, but when it becomes a pattern, then it becomes more serious. Never neglect it; never ignore it. Reach out. It might be one of the most difficult things you have to do, but reach out and let somebody else assist you, walk with you, and loan you his or her faith and hope at this time when yours is so low. That way you'll be able to get through it."

What to do if you feel suicidal:

1. Call 911 or go to the emergency room.

2. Call a friend, family member, doctor, pastor, or counselor immediately, and tell that person that you are feeling suicidal. You should not be alone.

3. Call a suicide help line, such as 1-800-273-TALK (8255). Keep these phone numbers by your telephone or saved in your cell phone.

The Bible includes many records of men and women crying to God in desperation and honesty. You can follow their example by reading their words as your prayer to God. A great example can be found in Psalm 61. Read these verses when you have time. For now, here's a prayer that you can cry out to God.

God, I'm overwhelmed. I don't like thinking or feeling the way I am right now, and I want all this to stop. Help me remember that You see my tears and hear my every thought. I am frozen and don't know what to do or whom to turn to. Help me to trust that You are with me, even now, and to trust there is no problem or situation too big for You to handle. Guide and direct me to the person or the help I need. Thank You for loving me, and thank You for the Bible because it points me to hope. In Jesus' name I pray. Amen.

RESOURCES

My DIVORCE Care
Free online holiday help

When Thanksgiving and Christmas roll around, you'll be glad for the extra tips and suggestions at MyDivorceCare. Check out the videos and articles on how to deal with issues people experiencing separation or divorce face during the holidays at **divorcecare.org/my.**

DivorceCare: Hope, Help, and Healing book

Gain strength for each day with these 365 short readings. You'll meet people in the book who know exactly what you're going through, and you'll gain daily tips and encouragement. Find *DivorceCare: Hope, Help, and Healing During and After Your Divorce* by Steve Grissom and Kathy Leonard at **divorcecare.org/devotional** and at popular online stores.

One Day at a Time free daily email messages

Wake up to a note of encouragement in your inbox by signing up for the free daily email messages, "One Day at a Time," at **divorcecare.org/dailyemails**. You can also email a friend who is hurting and encourage him or her to sign up. These messages are available in book form (see above).